MUSHARONA

Poems by Brett Underwood

Kung Fu Treachery Press
Rancho Cucamonga, CA

Copyright © Brett Underwood, 2020
First Edition: 1 3 5 7 9 10 8 6 4 2
ISBN: 978-1-952411-28-1
LCCN: 2020943037

Cover design by St. Louis illustrator Jerome Gaynor. Follow his work on Instagram @jeromez_weird_brain, or get copies of his freaky comic books of at www.weird-brain.com
Author photo: Jim McGowin
All rights reserved. No part of this publication may be
reproduced or transmitted in any form or by any means,
electronic or mechanical, including photocopying,
recording or by info retrieval system, without prior
written permission from the author.

Acknowledgments:

"FREEWRITING" appeared in *Lick My Squaggle Noose, Clam Tick*
"Yeah, I Know Appeared" in *Sunlit Insults*
"A Fine How-Do-You-Do That an Animal Won't Understand" Appeared in *Sunlit Insults*
"MASTICATION" Appeared on *52ndcity.com*

Thanks to Andee Champion and Andrew Cohen for their lines in "Cellphone Raps Beat Boredome".

TABLE OF CONTENTS

What I Would If Lived in Desert

The Spring of 2020 / 1

WE GOT THAT PANDEMIC!! / 3

Freewriting / 6

Be OR GO / 8

today that I listened to this or The Letter

   I'll Write After You Break My Heart / 9

Cellphone Raps Beat Boredome / 13

FOODLISH DECISIONS BECOME YOUR

   BURNING HEART / 14

Draw It to Know It / 15

Two Plus Two / 16

Empathy Much? / 17

He Stopped / 18

A Place to Do One's Thinking / 19

Back Yard / 21

Straight Down / 23

Cartographic Numbskulls / 24

Envision Light / 26

Haikus / 28

Yeah, I Know / 30

A Fine How-Do-You-Do / 31

Woopty Shit / 32

Ode to the Fanatics / 33

Chuck Barris Died for Your Sins / 35

Belch Garlic Winds / 39

Amidst it All / 40

Fade In Time / 41

There There Now / 42

Mastication / 44

What? / 48

Fixes Like the Angels of Hell / 50

Shave the Planet / 52

She Will or She Won't / 54

SUNLIT IN LUST / 56

SADNESS / 57

LIFE / 61

This one is for those who made me laugh and cry.
Those who drove me down and picked me up.
This one is for anyone and anything that ever drove me to the limit or back home.
This one is for anyone who ever fed and "watered" me, listened to me, taught me and drove me mad with a show of apathy and ignorance.
This one is for anyone who ever thought they loved or hated me with a marked conviction.
This one is for everyone who loved me for sure and forever and do now and will forever.

How long does it take a man to learn that he does not, cannot want what he "wants?" You have to be in Hell to see Heaven. Glimpses from the Land of the Dead, flashes of serene timeless joy, a Joy as old as suffering and despair.

–William S. Burroughs

Whenever you find yourself on the side of the majority, it is time to pause and reflect.

–Mark Twain

This has to be the first poetic thing I ever put on paper
(penmanship paper, 1st grade?)

WHAT I WOULD IF LIVED IN DESERT

If I were an animal in the desert
I would take nibbles of cactus until I got to the juice.
I would make a home of sticks.
I would hunt for food and water every day.
I would make a bed out of weeds.
But most of all I would die.
What would you do?

       –October 24, 1972

The Spring of 2020

The moment spoke.
Said, *Aww, Man. I gotta plan.*
Ain't gonna do shit as long
as I can so I can get something done
and figure out this world and what's left of life
and right about a mind in the world and figure
it out inside without the strictures of time.

When the birds can see the wisdom
of the universe between the clouds
in the eyes of the stars
bring more madness to ensue
before other bosses call
and it is time to get it all down.

Hear the moment.
Time to count the seconds of a minute
and examine the design
of a thought in a second,
meaning the beat of the heart
and there is no hurry,
but don't get run over.

Sure, the muscle cars are gunning
through the streets
and sales are high
and all the people are dying,

because, because, because,
because of the wonderful
things He does
and gunshots, too, of course.
Blam blam blam blam.

but...know don't know
the answer to each day and night
and don't know and know and let flow.

Lay low and let the answers
question gobs and oodles
of sounds and noodles,
suds and mayhem, too.
Lucky ones in this moment
dodge the bullshit and the bullets
and the deadly vapor.
Work and other foolishness will come to finish
you off again someday, Silly.

We Got That Pandemic!

Once in a while and a wow
something pulls me outta my grave
of days or the daze of mundane commentary
and joys in such or graves of days.
It is April in 2020.

There is a scene in the old series
of THE WIRE. It shows kids slingin'
on a Baltimore corner like paperboys
with carnie pitches.
"We got that Pandemic!!" they cry.

Oh, don't act like this is some kind of surprise,
you fucking Dweebs.
You knew it was coming.
You knew that I had to come out and ask.
So, Dorks,
give me ideas for a chord progression
for this ballad I'm working on called
"COCKBLOCKED BY CORONA".

Tonight, it was as simple
as a neighbor's porchlight going out
on a night when we couldn't do it together
and that gummy bear in the door
of the fridge found when I knocked
the salsa over in a sort of bliss.

Don't do something.
Don't try.
In sleep there are dreams.

Where was I?
Eh, I was lost, losing, scanning.
I was watching K. Curtis Lyle talk about Bob Kaufmann
on one screen and a Dallas poet commented
in a thread,
the Auden beauty, "As I Walked Out One Evening"
on another fucking reality
but All Right.

I walked out this morning
and into the afternoon
but popped my head out of a glass
and plopped my ass down in a chair
for a look at the night. The row.
The Street.

Breaths. Breathing. While pupils dilate.
Stretches of weary shoulders
taking in one day and imagining the next.

Looking up. A plethora of stars
even on this Dutchtown street
it was almost amazing, but nothing
like I have seen on other nights in the desert
of your heart or the vacant look in your eyes
or in vast canyons of the Yukon
or over the bushes which I pissed on in bliss
that is the void.

I still see the shine in your eye
and the confusion in the heart
of your jeans
when the grooves
were up in the air.

Look at this sky and realize why we are fucked.
Fucked because Blind.
Focused on the opposite of sacred.
Our faces in false light of screens.

Tonight, there is a comet or an asteroid shower
or something out there
but I'm not craning my neck for anything
other than epiphany
or the dumb thoughts between the stars
and that will do
and keep me out of the alleys.

In the end, what most amused me was the drone
hovering and sleuthing through the blur
to the southwest of the duplex
that I rent and as I spun up out of my chair
I flipped
the drone the bird, dumped
some more beer
into my face and went off to my nightmares.

Who knows?
In the morning, I might be giggling.

Freewriting

Freewriting happens when the fever takes over and the loss-of-sight hits your pen and the cops writing you a ticket and the Tylenol lets you lose sleep, but not breathe and a wrestling match with an IBM turns out to ruin your day. Four pages turns into a jumbled hell and the traffic on 270 seems like another blur along freedom's road to some slavery-induced caterwaul. Some caterwauling-Tylenol-freedom seduction is what the president is…some caterwauling-Tylenol freedom march is what school---what rush hour is…what you all are…what I am and why can't we just remain healthy because when we are we don't really need to send anything down our systems. We just complain that the pills are gone, that our permits for normalcy are expired…that the cops and the flu are gonna kill us all and it no longer matters what the propaganda fountains spew forth. We are all aching and coughing and sick of it all. The Tylenol has run out. The bottle runs low. The tires dig deep in the depths of black snow.

All I can bear to do is sleep and lie my head restlessly in a puddle of muck that remains on the horizon for me to eat when the trains are gone and the victims are the ones you love…when the aliens plug up all your life sources and tell you on TV that your life is better. Four swans on camera, but no one sees anything except what's on the gawddam screen. No one gets to see those swans for real. 'Cause the life suckers are here and they're never giving up what they have---power. Power and Tylenol and spit, vim and vigor.

They have a lust for life. Your life! We all just complain that the pills are gone, that the permits for normalcy are expired. We struggle so much with our expectations of what we're supposed to be and what they've told us we should be that we need those pills, those permits, those excuses.

To truly be ourselves we would be like nothing imaginable. We would not follow a plan and walk a walk, talk a talk or regiment ourselves. To truly be you, you would follow your desires. You would empty yourself and just react. You wouldn't do what a permit let you or what a pill made you feel like doing, or what a cop is pressuring you to do. You would do what you could at that very moment on into time because then you would see the happiness, the effect of your dreams. The logic of your soul. You would claw and scratch for your chance to get up and out there, wherever it is and you would then just go and flow no tempo…or maybe there would be a lot. We would not complain. We would do it ourselves. We would not know the word "normal".

Be Or Go

If you've never hung up
or been hung
up on by a suicidal waitress
and then eaten cold pizza
while pissing in the sink
thinking
of Miles of climate
changed Smoke
and looking at yourself
in the mirror
can you really say
You know
Who
You
Are
or where you
might be
or go?

today that I listened to this or The Letter I'll Write After You Break My Heart

Had a dream today that I listened to this
and maybe I was with Wilhelm Reich
and William S. Burroughs or maybe I simply
knew that they were listening from elsewhere/place/
time.
Like you do with a lot of other dreams after a few drams
(just a play on words, I don't measure my soma in such
measures)))))

Did we talk about the orgone generator
and The Mass Psychology of Fascism
only, or was there something else?

Fear, ignorance and control without soul?
Sorry.

You weren't part of my Saturday,
but I couldn't have had it if you were around.
The plant is thirsty.
The computer is like an undiscovered
step child locked in a cage
with a depressed pit bull.

Started writing a poem:
"If you read this with your pants on
and the headphones turned up

just a little further than your buzz
dial the boss and tell him
it is for the candy-colored bunions
of your stage coach Mammy.

Tell him you desire butterfly dust
in your milk bottles in the morning.
Tell him. Tell him. Tell him
there is no stain without shouting
and ape shit algebra.
Tell him you love him. Set him free."

Ha!

I don't know why.
This one flew in the window.
Down the street. Amidst sirens.
It is the sound of a lack of a stomach pump
and a blow job during Game 6
after a tough inning.
A castration of the masses.

The poppaloppers are eating junk food.
The voyeurs have choked on static.
Don't worry, I think of marriage and love as did Corso.
Of course, oh Why wear shows
like shoes.

Scream BUTTERFLY DUST!
at the cashier.
Music and cock roaches will dissolve their idiocy
into food if the fungus
doesn't do it first.

From the other side of summer,
answers are the veil of questioning.
Quietness sleeps and awakens the…
tells in the shadow.

Whispers in the wind.
Utterances in the mix.
Hopes for hopes
for hopes for happiness in gasping
breaths of doubt.

Doubt is the needed adversary of hope.
Belittles it.
Make it larger than belief.
Whispers truth that defines beauty.
Reveals wonder.
Doubt has you rest
in a bed of shadows.
It blankets you with the wind.
It utters lonely bedtime stories that take sleep away.

Maybe helps disrupt the lock on the electrical
whatchamacallits.
Beauty there betwixt light and dark.
In the spaces between what is and what is not.

Memories and imagination meet.
Dreams dissolve into tomorrow.
Fingers of what?
What did they touch.

Dreams belong to NOW.
Before tomorrow
takes away all imaginings.

Reaching fingers grasp hold.
Hesitant hands miss the catch.
Dreams are both striving and uncertain.
Dreams are beauty until they are gone.
There is only
Thought.

Cellphone Raps Beats Boredome

Brett texts:
Down down no way
I bet you got a new way?
Stuck in a bucket like a mop
with no name.
It's 108 and I forgot to buy soap.
You can lead a whore to culture
if you can't stand the Pope.
(Killing time waiting for bands to show up.)

Andee adds:
Smoke pulled the pork.
Hawaii shaved the ice.
Voodoo did the donuts.
And we all stayed weird.
(I'm in Portland, Aregon.)

Andy:
Limes, lemons, oranges never
foraged in a forest, pick them off
stickly arms of crackly, bony
porous/trees, we form and leave,
fuck formal authorities
we aim to sorta please these
crowds of forlorn feral forces..
*(110 in Tucson, playing an anarchist Circus in Phoenix
on Saturday, then on to the post-coast)*

Foodlish Decisions Become Your Burning Heart

I'm starting to realize that paradoxical
mud puppy scream that I had for breakfast
might come back to bite me
bite you
and the children of phonics
will pay no never mind to the guy
at the farmer's market who wants you to vote
for salad when all you want is a frankfurter
to be your daddy.

Woke, broke and mundane will drive you insane
quicker than my phone made out of rocks
and dinosaur bones.
So put another nickel in the broken
system and wait for nirvana to pay
your rent, rub you out and reach
around your flimsy hip to answer
your dopey aunt's prayers.

Draw It To Know It

When the Bossgod Blabber
King says it sounds like
Sartre, but to me if feels
like Bukkake
They got a lot of me.

Ha!

No. Ha! No they don't!

But let me tell you something:
free food is delicious

Also, in other news:
Closure is the new orifice
Pork is the new portal
Single is the new Hitler
and
Fuckdeather
is
not a
duckfeather.

Two Plus Two

Handwringing and defeatism
work through the madness
but it wouldn't be so bad
if they didn't use metaphors
for insults.

Is happiness more attachment?
Let's just cut the bullshit here.
To live in a state of burnout, ask:
"When wrestling met rock & roll. Who won?"

Empathy Much?

Do you yearn? In the melody of a suicide moon?
Or under the sun on a sacred mound
with oblivious tourists.
One must yearn
to do the trick after guitars and sunburn.

After the gristle from the burger is washed
down by the jug of wine/ After one leaves
and before the heartache is diminished/
When there is time to give the world
a little goosey goosey/
Wanting is not enough.
LUST is too much under the volcanic ash .
NEED.
Well, there is that...
Shit...
Reboot.

Did you boot?
Need is desperate.
The root of dire situations/
Corners crammed with the dispossessed.

Some people are not worried about immigrants.
They are on fire or under fire and fleeing the fuck
from flames.
They've got a buncha words for yearn.
What will you do when they look in your window?
Where do they go?

He Stopped

It was Monday afternoon
Bill was thinking of offing himself
in the freshly fallen
snow when two crows
flew over head
Their black against the intense
Whiteness sky
and didn't know why
anymore, so he walked into the park
and filled his lungs with cold glass
air
to keep him in the life.

A Place to Do One's Forgetting

On one of those horrid late-Winter Saturdays,
Bead People in designer jeans, diamond rings
on their fat fingers, walk
like it is painful, waddling
in their muumuus and beads

They pray over their deli sandwiches
in a pub playing rock
in a place you'd never imagine that
to happen
In a place you were visiting
to avoid such things
this
this
Why?

Makes it easy
to walk out after two pints

On Tuesday afternoon, however, Nick Cave
is on the speakers, growling
over two rockers necking
in between tequila sips

At THE CROW'S NEST, "THE WARRIORS"
is projected on one wall and Lemmy
hangs over the bar patrons and booth inmates

on the opposite wall
while the chicken tacos
are stabbed through on a plate
next to a coffee stout
and John Dorsey's *Appalachian Frankenstein*
pages forgives us all

All of it so beautiful
you forget about war
and suicide for a minute

Back Yard

As the squirrels skitter
manically
up a three-story tree
and the birds
sing their horny songs
I remember the skin
The faces
of friends
talking about suicide
The ones that happened
Another that was just
entertaining the thought

And spooning
after too much whiskey
and smoke.

Memories
In the bed
In the bathtub
Or a joyous bike ride
And rain in
a hammock

There was that

Kisses
There were kisses

And rain
Red wine
The wisdom of that
and kisses

Kisses and the whispers
Of wind through the leaves.

Straight Down

Most of the raindrops
fall straight
down
from a silent
sky
today
on a Sunday
when nothing
seems to coax
logic.

But there are dozens
more
of these drops
running North along
along the neighbors'
lines
like tram cars
until they fall to the ground
just off the deck.

I imagine
the catastrophes unknown.
while a squirrel chuckles
into the gurgling drain.

Cartographic Numbskulls

Knowing that the butt
is aflame
after the failure of journalism
in a cool, stiff rain
under a broken limb
in a foreign forest

It is nice
to walk the sidewalks
of a broken world
of misspelled verbs
and broken promises.

After a meal
of unscrambled segues
and dog food
amidst the babble
of the diner attendants
and unimaginative dolts
or a view of the wet,
slick streets alive with oil
and broken neon,

It is nice
to walk home
through the corpses
and have a quiet and lonely

wank and fall silently
asleep on a dirty carpet
of comfort knowing
the rent is due.
The seed is spent.
The credit is overdue
until the next Googlemaps
nightmare to get to that place
of awakening a defecation
taste in the parking
lot could not care less.

Envision Light

Still in socks on a November night,
but the computer blows warm air
on legs and the hood is over head
as it bows over a Damian Rucci
poem about ex-girlfriends
becoming strangers and the disruptive
and powerful forces of change
and then comes a fruit fly in search
of the missing whiskey glass
that should be on the desk.
It foolishly lands on page 5
and crawls towards the left margin.
I crush it there, re-open the book
and turn the page.

In a few minutes, the computer crashes
and it is time scribbled into the script
before the director closes the set
for another take. Another scene.
to hit the streets for the missing whiskey.

Nothing is certain.
Still time to talk to the dead
and whatever life can be

Oh, take it back to a land of forgiveness
and hope where limbs break
under the weight of nooses
and become wings.

Where tweets of anger beget
wisdom and urgency sleeps
in siestas in a warm breeze and bullets
turn into fleas that buzz music
in golden rays.

Where open eyes envision light
and gravity lapses into strength.

And Now, It Is Time For Haikus

PYTHON
Dear Mister Python
You're hugs are not nice. They're mean.
You made my shit list.

YAK
Single, slutty Yak
Sun bakes the cum on your back
As you graze alone

CHIMPANZEE
Motherfucking Chimp
Has a chip on his shoulder
Gives your Mom the Aids

LAMB
God-fearing Lamb
Will not go out on a limb
Is riddled with guilt

ZEBRA
Herpes-Scarred Zebra
Schizophrenic and starving
Anticipates death

CHIHUAHUA
Pus-filled eye sockets
Deaf, lame Chihuahua
Licks his ball all day

TRICERATOPS
Yo, Triceratops!
Lick my sweaty balls
Flick me through the sky

HUMAN HAM BOUNTY
Your necrotic flesh
Envelopes a ham sandwich
You are paralyzed

Yeah, I Know

Yeah, I know
The excuses that he made
'cause you're the leper!
Take off that face!

A Fine How-Do-You-Do That an Animal Won't Understand

Why don't you pull
a sumac branch out of
your innuendo;
Sit on your own face;
And I'll fuck your god in
the heart
with a pear and pepper
chutney gunspasm.

Woopty Shit!

As for the pre-cum
of the original fucker,
did he see a sunset
and make it before he
did fire?
See the joke before
the demise of his actions?
Stop one throw of one rock
before the first cock
thrust into the first
cunt of creation
degredation of
humanity shit
on the dirt?
What if he used that
hotshot thumb of his to hold
back that hearty splooge?
What if?
Just for instance…
No air-conditioners, yep.
No Maury Povich, yep.
No Trump tweets
Or dead in the streets.
No lawyers, yep.
Yep.
Yep.
Yep.
Shoot it back into the dust.
Cry until there is mud between your broken toes.

Ode To The Fanatic

Funny racism or runny fascism while
ye prisoners of hope and fall colors
eat pumpkin-spiced cold meds and mucous to
avoid neti pot death hot dogs and waitresses
flying in every direction.
Put wastoids in your booster
Club gravitas.
Load ether with lead-ladened muchmuck.
Cough up gravy into your designer tissue.

Oh, and Ichabod's head is off the top
of the visitor's dugout and kangarooing
up the aisle in that horse's ass.
Van hit the soybean head
shoot dead boy stranger danger
inexperienced eagle gorged on afterbirth
of your denial.

Root for the one percent in your muumuu.
Chug aluminum –bottled water and hoot.
Live it up. Toss lewd verses to garbage.
Your days are few. Your wool is worthless.
Replay these days and they'll go back and look at it
stored on yourtube or reflected in a mirror coffin
or another threat to the environment babbling
DADA in a six-wheeled stroller.

Would that we could all slip on our corporate muumuus and waddle into the stadium with such unity. Oh
inner thigh sweat that melds with nacho cheese, scraped off with a $175 ticket stub purchased with corporate funds.

Chuck Barris Died For Your Sins

Gotta box lunch now
in the fascism rain.
The best movies
on the phone and
the theatre
closed.
History and hysteria
fuck in the dust
and we've got more stuff.

The ejaculate stream
on the airwaves spits
its poison
into the vacant minds of
of the blind, toothless
eagle cooks are driving
because there's more traffic.
History and hysteria fuck
in the dust in the memory
of Jay P. Morgan's
wicked grin.

The tweeters
wouldn't know a good film
if it bit them on the tip
of their underfed
jizztubes.

Dust in their muscles
a hysterical muck.

Meanwhile, the jackhammer
rains suicide breakfast
for those who crave sunshine
and the lavatory attendants
scream into the raindrop
soup of sycophantic convulsions
about the fantasy conventions
of peaking into toilet stalls
the thought of memory:
history and hysteria
fuck in the dust.

The hooker pumps like
Alan Hale, the skipper
from Gilligan's Island.
Arms all akimbo
to put her corpulence in
motion that her legs
alone won't muster.
History and hysteria fuck
in the dust.

Down the street
to hustle for anything
but another trick
that requires walking funny
into another broken-glass morning's

desperate operations
for a cheap, foodless
meal for a fuck
in the dust.

Daylight is burning
and nights are wasted.
Tasted like cemetery mounds
for those left in the places
where there is still
something like there there
in the high school halls
where we dreamt of topless
barbers who refused dates
pulling the high note
down from the Arctic circle
with a spastic colon.

Not the patting on the back;
not consolation.
Leave the streets to their
commerce or erase the soul
while history and hysteria
fuck in the dust.

Can't move to Canada.
While history and hysteria
fuck in the dust,
but we can break those
tea cups and throw away
those spoons.

While history and hysteria
fuck in the dust
and if life's a bowl
of cherries
then what's death?
an avocado?

(snickering…oh….no…….no
No
No no no no no no no no no no no no no no
Aren't you something?

Belch Garlic Wind

In wonder if you can shit
without sunshine from your eyes
then kiss the slobber from forgotten trumpets
belted out of the ignorance of beer bottles and caverns.

Polish the door knob of a Jungian missile
to be sure the music emits magic
in the darkness, keys tinkling
the sadness and plaintive hope
of birds and nothingness, making it O.K.
to slumber despite injustice, poison and violence.

Sleep beauty. Paint pictures.
Blend colors and words.
Emit light.

Answer your fears with boldness.
Belch garlic wind into the flames.
Give up hope.
Sleep.

Amidst It All

While the waitresses worry about chem trails,
the tine punctures the yoke.
The oxen fire off salvos.
The surgeon butchers a joke.
The nurses snort the last of the blow.
The Malamute barks at the skunk.
The busboy is suffering grief and sore feet.
The priest is discovering Punk.
The clouds are a fluttering afterthought,
though daily, they blot out the sun.
The dirt drinks the rain and the blood of
The masses
and you think you're the only one.

Come trade me your woes for a job full of blows
and a dozen obsequious morons.
I'll smile at your face, let you win the race
and scoff at your enemy pawns.

Fade in Time

Cover the garden soil
with man whose worth
is otherwise under question
(but for a well-defined palate)
until said activity lifts him
from no ego to danger junky,
smothering life whimsically
and rotting from within
simultaneously
man-become-life-manure-become-enabler
sole.

Pecking, pecking, pecking
away at sweet nothings.
Luckily, tiny bruises fade in time
and the bartender is spent.
His building is empty
and his stereo speakers
are doing the pouring.

There There Now

Buried behind those eyes and quivering lips
there is a question waiting to emerge.

To murder or go out to breakfast
before work or run for the hills
are two options looming.

The psychotic lapdog has no way of knowing
the depth of your confusion and hatred.

The cellulite in the thighs of the owner
grows with fear, though we live only steps

from a fabulous park. A relentless bark
from a tortured Doxie.

Part of a conversation
talkin' 'bout dolcimers
pair well with mushroom gravy

talkin' bout masturbation
is essential

Shit, Man. This bar tab equation.
That sound like "J" and "Z" are drunk.

Little bitch runs me outta the hizzy.
Oughta know better by now,
but her teeth can't be shoved or showed.

The way they torture a tired man
in a tired life in a tired bed
Refusing to nozzle or leash
 her to quell the yips" should be
The way they torture a tired man
in a tired life in a tired bed
refusing to nozzle or leash her
to quell the yips,

Gonna go DEXTER some day
if I ever quit wondering why.

Mastication

It wasn't always like this: your mind: scrambled eggs with ketchup. At times when you were alive and sure of it, you're senses were on fire. You pulled off the highway just as they were dulled and found the perfect place to do what humans do.
Consume.
And you did.
The booths were empty and you took your pick.

There was time to settle in and take a sip of that first cup of coffee. It was the first you'd allowed yourself in 900 miles, since an incident with a deer under your rig and then a bored game warden who kept ogling your teenage hitchhiker.
Hey, I'm gonna eat this apple and let you tell the story.

O.K.
So I'm in this cheeseball diner somewhere in the western part of Mississippi.
Fuckin' Eightball Soup, Mississippi.
There is enough clucking going on in this fucking henhouse that you can sense a symphony in the sound of this commune off-the-road, and just when you are about to set it to a beat of your Kenworth crossing the struts in the highway, an exchange takes your fancy.

"You won't break the rules," this bitch with his back to my booth says, when the buck-toothed carrot-top waiter approached him. I mean this fucker was skinny and orange and had fucking green hair. I heard his sleeve rip a bit as his sneakers screeched to a halt and coffee cups clacked together.

"I'm sorry," the gopher apologized in mock defense as he mentally mounted an offense against his urge to quell an assault before barking, "What?"

"Food," this stinky fucker behind me said, "You promised food."

At this point, imagine it is a 1970s radio spot from someone like the fatman, Charles Kuralt. The voice that buttered your pancakes and made it O.K. that you didn't finish your oatmeal while the VC mounted sinewy attacks and your Mom plopped around the kitchen in a stupid fucking muumuu and a perm.

"The sign says "food," the cat says, sounding like the fat man.

Get the warmth of the voices, though this may seem like an odd repartee. But the exchanges will lose all of their hostility if they are imagined in such a tone. They drip down over your blueberry waffles like hot Aunt Jemima as if you've blotted out that part of your brain that responds to the fight-or-flight instinct.

"Yes," the waiter said, taking a step back and like this, releasing his sleeve from the clutches of the stranger and shining a cute glimpse at the wackjob.

"Then?"

"Reformed milksops clamber for cous cous and Emmy Hennings craves kelp, Sir."

"I shall return to fill your needs." this booger-topped Q-tip says, though I admit that he skillfully donned a smirk and was off.

Shit, Man! Take it easy on that apple. I'm tryin' to tell a story over here.

So I can hear this freak behind me steaming.

"Give me what the cannibals are having," he's thinking and fuming, his fingers now digging for a cheap smoke or perhaps the fabric clinging at the space between his buttocks as he fidgets, causing the silverware to clatter against my water glass.

Anyway, motherfucker finally settles down and I was able to do so myself.

Now, were it not for my hunger and curiosity, you might, at this point, think that I turned to the gentleman and asked if he'd like a bite of my Twinky, but instead I asked myself which film of the 99 that they shot about Glenn Gould this enchilada most reminded me of, and while I'm wondering, the billboard shining above my truck changed to indicate that rice was at a dangerously low level…and I really was wondering whether the menu offered Moo Goo Gai Pan, that gentle chicken dish that tends to ease my gastrointestinal woes on many a trip like that one…and besides, I had eaten that Twinky in my dreams east of Fresno yesterday morning. So, my hunger and the coffee are in mad communion and all I see on the menu is grease.

Another face is in mine now and I hear myself order, "Jello with whipped cream, I guess."

"Green or red?" the face asked.

"Green", I muttered while remembering your mother's garden…and all those cucumbers. Geez dude!
What the
fuck?

Man, this is a good apple.

Man, shut the fuck up, I'm tellin' a story. You said so.

All right, all right. Go ahead.

Aw, fuck it. I'm hungry. You wanna go to Sloppy's?

Oh yeah! Let's chow!

What?

..Sit
don't go down.
Smile
don't know
frown.
Wrap those lips
around my
finger now,
Clown.

Ditch
that
Sun Down.
Don't
cry, Honey now.
Release the grip
around my finger.
There's a full moon
spilled with peach.
There's a shutdown
that I won't reach.

Moonlight shares
a common ground
with shade your being's
in.

Tear that shine
away to
see a dark side.
Tear that burning pole
and get a wet slide---
lunge and stride
at the end
where reward
lies.

Fixes Like the Angel of Hell

Delegating the pencil
to the crapper, the tweets
and hawks took over obliterating
justice in favor of the correct

There were no proofreaders and
spellcheckers and the pawns
thought they could hump kings
and that's ridiculous and they

ran stop signs and that was fun
and they popped locks and
snapped shots and posed much

but it made them obvious
and they ended in the cages and
were convinced that they were
in the cages and they didn't get
out they didn't
get out and they didn't get off

But they could have
If the concentration had been more like
The truth

My memory of you looking out the window
at the beauty of the sunset
appreciation of the third glass of wine.

Turned head for a minute
Maybe it was that prick next door
she was eyeballin'?

But the breeze, the buzz and the aroma
Of the moment
The Truth.

Shave the Planet

Annoying fakes yearn for the babble
and bill-yourself puppets incite
the direct result
of the agitated driver
objects,
possibly rocks
purse and passport
nice apples
nasty pigs
Thick smells, musty and fetid
wonderful subdivision
sound like sandy-eared ostriches
chicken, motor oil, and herpes
from close-range discharge
an old showman smell of sickness
and sound reality snow mysticism
leaving muscleman in the back
seat of the car for 4.5 minutes

Utah means packed powder
The ocean. The ruins.
notice the moon and the sun
tombstones like parties with mylar balloons
baited by the troll that
cops beat & kidnapped,
blending logical fallacies.
considered important because he is "neutral."

God loves, his bitch litters
it's known as the suicide belt
of accusatory side eye
too early in the morning.

In an uncomfortable opposition
to Anaïs Nin come pooping
while Hoosiers stun Missouri
normative articulateness formative
shots from a loaded turkey sandwich
from leading anti-science activists
up the bum 'fore a new election or
a new erection of excision, trimming, re-arranging
moldy teddy bears and sarcasm-enraged Nazis
under a helicopter sky
to mourn provocative targets .

She Will or She Won't

He is not the sun.
He is not the moon.
He and she are dust.
They want to be rock.
Wanting to be the stars in eyes.
Wanting to stun with sparks
in lips and lightning
between thighs.

Don't want to lie
but wanting to lie down
with the truth
and here is the problem:
They are broken
and quite a bit afraid.
Animals cry themselves to sleep
with wanted nipples
in their collective lips.

Can you come sweetly
like you don't know that is such?

Can you horn in on continents from the center
and know that the cock and the cunt
have built this world?
There is only asking the world of that knowledge.
There are no other takers and givers.

That, imagine, from seeing and hearing
and hoping what any woman
can be for herself and being a savior
at the same time
doesn't add up.

Sober time?
Know that is fucking ridiculous
but know what excites, tingles
and sometimes scares.

Your heart. Your voice.
To be rebuilt stroke by stroke.
Mother Earth.

Heart is MUSH.
If it isn't fed, it might shit it into the woods
or hurl it back into the sky.

Sunlit in Lust

Green, yellow, brown, bright,
Sure.
I miss the terribly, beautiful
Sunsets.
Red, orange steaming heat
Yeah.
That's part of IT.
Breezes and bicycles
Flowing skirts and leaves blowing
Hot dogs and horses
All right.

But I like the gray
The monochromatic
and the subtle hints.
And I know that all those colors
are captured in the ONE:
The white light.
I like the magic
in a screaming snowball
in the night
All the colors in that jagged
orb.
That is where I am headed.
That glaring sunlight
of one circle
The gross of pain and love.
Take me there.

Sadness

Sadness
takes its pants off
Sadness
right away
Sadness
Pitter patter
Sadness
Snores today
Sadness
Sees another rain
Sadness
down the drain

Sadness
takes a wrong turn
Sadness
dumb and gray
Sadness
turns to loneliness
Sadness
steals the dream
Sadness
in the checkout line
Sadness
splits a seam
Sadness
in the sack

Sadness
fears the word
Sadness
wastes another dime
Sadness
off the rack
Sadness
needs another
Sadness
Shit is wack.

Sadness
got that hangdog look
Sadness
pays the bills
Sadness
takes another sip
Sadness
sometimes swills
Sadness
works it extra hard

Sadness
fucks off daily
Sadness
looks it in the eye
Sadness
makes the kills
Sadness
reaps a tear drop
Sadness
Now and then

Sadness
dreams of other times

Sadness
Sadness
Sadness

Sadness
Just a little more
Sadness
All or none
Sadness
puts it on the line
Sadness
in the store
Sadness
knows no better
Sadness
on the shore

Sadness
bakes it in a pie
Sadness
might as well
Sadness
missed the bus
Sadness
kissed the whore
Sadness
hits the big time
Sadness
what the hell

Sadness
on the bar stool
Sadness
in the well
Sadness
on the television

Sadness
Sadness
Sadness

Sadness
takes another pill
Sadness
hits the vein
Sadness
on the grocery list
Sadness
likes the pain
Sadness
got another flat
Sadness
just goes shopping
Sadness
shrugs the shoulders
Sadness
ties a knot
Sadness
looks you in the eye
Sadness
marks the spot.

LIFE

EXISTEXISTEXISTEXISTEXIST
EXISTEXISTEXISTEXISTEXIST
EXISTEXISTEXISTEXISTEXIST
EXISTEXISTEXISTEXISTEXIST
EXISTEXISTEXISTEXISTEXIST
EXISTEXISTEXISTEXISTEXIST
EXISTEXISTEXISTEXISTEXIST
EXISTEXISTEXISTEXISTEXIST
EXISTEXISTEXISTEXISTEXIST
EXISTEXISTEXISTEXISTEXIST
EXISTEXISTEXISTEXISTEXIST
EXISTEXISTEXISTEXISTEXIST
EXISTEXISTEXISTEXISTEXIST
EXISTEXISTEXISTEXISTEXIST
EXISTEXISTEXISTEXISTEXIST
EXISTEXISTEXISTEXISTEXIST
EXISTEXISTEXISTEXISTEXIST
EXISTEXISTEXISTEXISTEXIST
EXISTEXISTEXISTEXISTEXIST
EXISTEXISTEXISTEXISTEXIST
EXISTEXISTEXISTEXISTEXIST
EXISTEXISTEXISTEXISTEXIST
EXISTEXISTEXISTEXISTEXIST
EXISTEXISTEXISTEXISTEXIST
EXISTEXISTEXISTEXISTEXIST
EXISTEXISTEXISTEXISTEXIST
EXISTEXISTEXISTEXISTEXIST
EXISTEXISTEXISTEXISTEXIST

EXISTEXISTEXISTEXISTEXIST
EXISTEXISTEXISTEXISTEXIST
EXISTEXISTEXISTEXISTEXIST
EXISTEXISTEXISTEXISTEXIST
EXISTEXISTEXISTEXISTEXIST
EXIT

Brett Lars Underwood has been published by *The Bicycle Review, 52ndcity, Bad Jacket, Bad Shoe, U City Review* and included in *Flood Stage: An Anthology of Saint Louis Poets*, both *Gasconade Reviews; 39 Feet and Rising, Missouri is a Ghost-Shaped Thing* and *After the Flood* (Spartan Press, 2019). His verse can also be found in his chapbook *Sunlit Insult* and *It's Bush Lent Subtle Hints. MUSH* from Spartan Press hit the streets in February, 2018. His work has been heard at the Pulitzer Foundation for the Arts' "Sound Waves" series and is part of Laumeier Sculpture Park's "Site/Sound" exhibit.